This book was purchased
with funds from a
generous donation by

Dr. Kathryn W. Davis

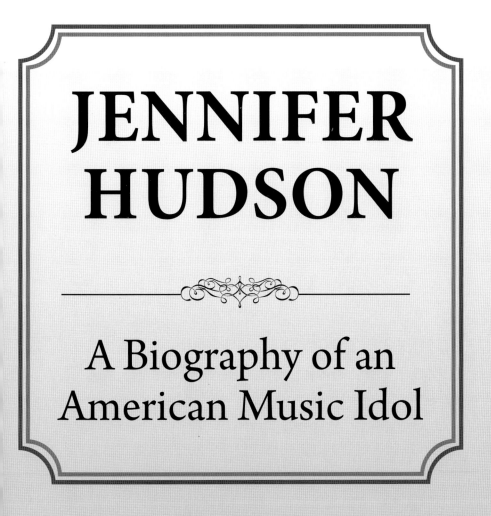

JENNIFER HUDSON

A Biography of an American Music Idol

John Micklos, Jr.

Enslow Publishers, Inc.
40 Industrial Road
Box 398
Berkeley Heights, NJ 07922
USA

http://www.enslow.com

Library of Congress Cataloging-in-Publication Data
Micklos, John.
  Jennifer Hudson : a biography of an American music idol / John Micklos, Jr.
    pages cm. — (African-American icons)
  Includes bibliographical references and index.
  Summary: "Examines the life of Jennifer Hudson, including her childhood in Chicago, her rise to superstardom from American Idol contestant to Grammy and Academy award winner, her family life, and her music and movie career"—Provided by publisher.
  ISBN 978-0-7660-4233-9
  1. Hudson, Jennifer, 1981—Juvenile literature. 2. Singers—United States—Biography—Juvenile literature. 3. Motion picture actors and actresses—United States—Biography—Juvenile literature. I. Title.
  ML3930.H82M53 2014
  782.42164092—dc23
  [B]
                    2013001337

Future editions:
Paperback ISBN: 978-1-4644-0409-2
EPUB ISBN: 978-1-4645-1224-7
Single-User PDF ISBN: 978-1-4646-1224-4
Multi-User PDF ISBN: 978-0-7660-5856-9

Printed in the United States of America
112013 Lake Book Manufacturing, Inc., Melrose Park, IL
10 9 8 7 6 5 4 3 2 1

To Our Readers:
We have done our best to make sure all Internet addresses in this book were active and appropriate when we went to press. However, the author and the publisher have no control over and assume no liability for the material available on those Internet sites or on other Web sites they may link to. Any comments or suggestions can be sent by e-mail to comments@enslow.com or to the address on the back cover.

♻ Enslow Publishers, Inc., is committed to printing our books on recycled paper. The paper in every book contains 10% to 30% post-consumer waste (PCW). The cover board on the outside of each book contains 100% PCW. Our goal is to do our part to help young people and the environment too!

Cover Illustration: AP Images / Charles Sykes / Invision.

CONTENTS

1. A Fateful Vote 5

2. Finding Her Voice 8

3. Making Music 17

4. "An Idol Tale" 29

5. Dream Role in *Dreamgirls* 42

6. Heartbreak and Hope 57

7. Role Model 71

   Chronology 95

   Chapter Notes 98

   Glossary 100

   Further Reading
   (Books and Internet Addresses) 101

   Index 102

Chapter 1

A Fateful Vote

J ennifer Hudson and Fantasia Barrino held hands and waited. Despite their masterful singing performances and praise from the judges, they were the two lowest vote getters on Top 7 week, season three of the smash-hit reality television show *American Idol*. Silently, they waited for the verdict.

Viewers were stunned by this result. At the beginning of the elimination evening, *Idol* host Ryan Seacrest had divided six of the remaining seven finalists into two groups. Group A included La Toya London, Jennifer Hudson, and Fantasia Barrino.

These three singers, all African Americans, had earned praise from the judges and were also audience favorites. Their big voices and bubbly personalities had earned them the nickname the "Three Divas."

In Group B stood John Stevens, Diana DeGarmo, and Jasmine Trias. Most critics felt these three, although talented, didn't quite match the others. The seventh contestant, George Huff, waited anxiously to see where he would be sent.

Seacrest told Huff to go stand with the top group. Huff hesitated just an instant before joining Barrino, Hudson, and London. Then, in one of the most dramatic *Idol* moments ever, Seacrest informed Huff that he was in the wrong group. From among the millions of votes cast that week by viewers throughout the United States, the "Three Divas" were the lowest vote getters. He told Huff to join the other group.

The audience buzzed as the news sank in. Barrino laughed in disbelief. Hudson simply looked stunned. Next, Seacrest told London that she was safe. Barrino and Hudson had the two lowest vote totals. One of them would be eliminated, and the other would survive to continue competing. Whose *Idol* dream was about to end? Like the rest of America, Barrino and Hudson waited nervously.

As always, Seacrest drew out the drama. He said the vote difference between the two was the smallest in *Idol* history. Then, finally, he announced that the person going home was . . . Jennifer Hudson.[1]

Emotions flooded her body. On the one hand, she firmly believed she had the talent to remain. On the other hand, the stress of living out the *American Idol* experience for so many weeks had taken a toll on her. "I wasn't upset," she later said in her autobiography, *I Got This: How I Changed My Ways and Lost What Weighed Me Down.* "I wasn't disappointed. To be totally honest, I felt relieved."[2]

Most of all, Hudson felt grateful. *American Idol* had been the once-in-a-lifetime opportunity to showcase her singing skills for a worldwide audience for six weeks.

Hudson and Barrino embraced. The judges looked somber. Several of the other contestants were close to tears. The audience gave Hudson a warm standing ovation.

"I knew in my gut that winning *American Idol* wasn't what God had planned for me," she later recalled. She knew that the experience would prepare her for whatever came next. Little did she know just how extensive those triumphs and tragedies would be.

Chapter 2

FINDING HER VOICE

T he little girl's voice filled the church. Worshippers could hardly believe that such a big, sweet, pitch-perfect voice could come from such a young girl.

Born on September 12, 1981, in Chicago, Illinois, Jennifer Kate Hudson began singing in public at the ripe old age of seven. She joined the Pleasant Gift Missionary Baptist Church choir, where she sang with her grandmother and the other choir members. The little girl with the big voice seemed able to master any song.

"I knew at the age of 7 what I wanted to do—that's when I started going after that dream, and I never looked back," she later said on her Web site.

Early on singing with the choir, she sought the spotlight as a soloist. At first, the other choir members resisted. They did not think such a little girl could handle such a big role. "They would never give me a solo or give me a chance, so I remember sitting in the bathroom at home crying, like, 'If nobody will listen to me sing, I'll listen to me sing,'" she told the *Chicago Tribune* in 2006.

Over time, the other choir members changed their minds. They could tell Jennifer had a special voice. Years later, she clearly recalled her first solo song: "Must Jesus Bear the Cross Alone?"

She recalled her excitement as she prepared for the first real opportunity to showcase her singing before an audience. She also remembered how nervous she got when the moment arrived. "I forgot the words, and the congregation had to help me out," she told the *Chicago Tribune* in 2006.

Singing in the choir also helped develop the unique vocal style that would define her voice into adulthood. Church music "teaches you how to connect to your music emotionally and make whatever you're singing have substance," Hudson said in a 2008 interview in *Chicago Magazine*. "That's the most meaningful place to sing from, when you're actually singing about something."

She also grew up admiring singers with big voices. When she was eleven, Whitney Houston released "I Will Always Love You." Dolly Parton had first made this song famous in 1974 as a simple country tune. Houston did a big-voiced, dramatic version that became a huge hit, spending fourteen weeks at number one on the *Billboard* charts. Hudson recalls singing along to the song at home. She didn't do the melody, though. She sang harmony and did it as a duet. She has cited Aretha Franklin and Patti LaBelle as her other big musical influences.

Hudson grew up in the Englewood section on the South Side of Chicago. The area has long been known for poverty, violence, and street crime. In fact, the neighborhood, which includes roughly a 20-block by 20-block area, saw 60 homicides in 2011. This is more than half the number of the entire city of Washington, D.C., that same year.[1]

Still, Hudson felt safe growing up. Her childhood home at 7019 South Yale Avenue was modest but clean. The white two-story single-family dwelling had a small yard and an iron fence out front.

"It was a decent neighborhood," she said in a 2007 interview published in the *London Evening Standard*.

"We were poor, but we thought we were rich, because we had everything we needed."[2]

Jennifer was the youngest of three children. Her nickname was Jenny Kate. Her older siblings, Jason and Julia, looked out for her. Early on, they realized her ambition. "All Jennifer wanted to do was sing and be famous," Julia told music network VH1 in 2010.

Jennifer enjoyed a happy childhood, although she rarely speaks of her father. In her autobiography, she simply says, "I am the third child of my parents, Darnell Hudson Donerson and Samuel Simpson. My mama raised me, my sister Julia, and my brother Jason on her own as a single parent."

Donerson worked as a secretary. Simpson drove a bus and died of cancer when Jennifer was a teenager. The family never had extra money, although Jennifer has said that they did sometimes take trips to other states.

Still, money was tight. In her autobiography, Hudson recalls that whenever she asked her mother for money, she only got a quarter. Her grandfather, who worked at a gas station, would give each of the children three dollars when he got paid. Then Jennifer felt she could buy anything.

Although her family may not have had a lot of money, Donerson kept the Hudson children busy with a variety of activities. James took piano lessons.

Jennifer did ballet. She also modeled for the Sears catalog when she was five. Most of all, she just loved to sing.

She also loved to spend time with family. She still does. As a child, Jennifer enjoyed the attention of a large extended family of aunts, uncles, and cousins. She felt especially close to her mother's parents.

Their shared love of music created a special bond between Jennifer and her grandmother, Julia Kate Hudson. Her grandmother was a talented singer who often performed solos for the church choir. Jenny Kate spent many happy hours singing at her grandma's house. She also loved to listen to her grandmother do gospel songs. One favorite was "How Great Thou Art." "My grandmother is where I got my voice from," she later told VH1.

Her grandmother was the one who brought her into the church choir as a girl. Jennifer looked forward to attending choir practice with her every Tuesday evening. She loved her grandmother's "belting, bluesy, gospel-tinged voice." The older woman served as a role model for her singing.

Many of Jennifer's childhood memories revolve around three things: singing, family, and food. Family and food often went together. The Hudsons enjoyed sharing time together, especially over meals. "It gave my mama a lot of joy to make meals for her kids,"

Jennifer wrote in her autobiography. Her mother especially enjoyed making a hot breakfast before sending her children off to school.

The weekly schedule also revolved around meals. The family feasted on homemade spaghetti every Wednesday. Every Friday they ate fried fish.

Jennifer looked forward to Sundays most of all. After attending church in the morning, the family went out for lunch. It was the only time that they ate out. Jennifer's mother and grandmother liked Kentucky Fried Chicken. The kids preferred McDonald's, so the family usually ate there. Jennifer generally ordered a cheeseburger with no onions. To this day, she dislikes onions.

The highlight of the day was Sunday dinner. "Sunday nights were full-on family-style dinners with all the fixings," Hudson later recalled in her autobiography. The family feasted on pork chops, fried chicken, mashed potatoes, macaroni and cheese, collard greens, and more. Dessert often featured peanut butter cookies and pound cake that was so rich that Hudson later said it should have been called "two pound cake."

That love of food helped contribute to Hudson growing up as a plus-sized girl, which proved to be both a curse and a blessing to her career over time. At the time, she didn't think much about it. Compared to her brother, sister, and mother, she was downright skinny. And most of the older girls in the neighborhood were full figured. "In the neighborhood I'm from in Chicago, a size 16 is normal," she later told *Self* magazine.

Over time, as Hudson grew taller and heavier and gained her own curves, she developed a distinctive style of dressing as well. "As I gradually gained weight, I started to develop my own way of dressing," she recalled. "I liked to call it 'free style.' I chose clothes I liked, not things that were trendy or name brands."

As a child, Jennifer showed both musical and artistic talent. Able to draw whatever she saw, she soon filled her bedroom with pencil sketches. She told people that she had her grandma's voice and her mother's artistic talent.

Young Jennifer also had a gift for pranks. She constantly played tricks on her family. Her mother found her kidding funny. She thought it indicated a talent and said she thought Jennifer might become an actress someday. Little did she know just how accurate that prediction would become.

But Jennifer's main focus was always singing. "Once I discovered music, I knew this was what I wanted to do," she told *Essence* magazine in 2011. "I haven't looked back."

Over time, more and more people told her she had a "gift." In addition to singing at church, she began entering—and usually winning—local talent shows. People from all over Chicago came to hear her.

"There was a certain sense of power that came with capturing my audience that left me wanting more," Hudson wrote in her autobiography. "They say that most performers live for the applause. Even as a little girl I understood what that meant, and the more I got, the more I wanted."

When Jenny Kate was about thirteen, her grand-mother suffered a stroke. After that, Jennifer spent much of her free time keeping her company. She even composed her first song, "To Love Somebody," to let her grandmother know how much she loved her.

Jennifer didn't do a lot of things that most teens around her did. She had a boyfriend, but they went to different schools, so she didn't spend a lot of time with him. She didn't hang out with girlfriends or go to movies and parties. She preferred to spend her free time with her family or singing. In a neighborhood where many teens turned to alcohol or drugs, Jennifer avoided those temptations. She kept her focus on her singing.

At eighth grade graduation, Jenny Kate had a solo. She sang Bette Midler's classic "Wind Beneath My Wings." She cried all the way through. Maybe she was thinking about her ill grandmother. Maybe she was sad about moving on to a new stage of her life.

Julia Kate Hudson died when Jennifer was sixteen. Since that time, Jennifer has always carried a heart-shaped stone as a remembrance.

"I vowed that I would go on with my life, follow my dream, and make good decisions along the way so I would make her proud," Jennifer later said. And her dream was just beginning to unfold.

Chapter 3

MAKING MUSIC

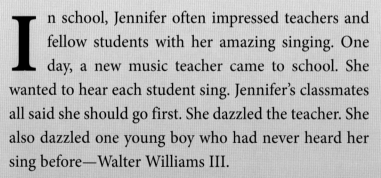

I n school, Jennifer often impressed teachers and
fellow students with her amazing singing. One
day, a new music teacher came to school. She
wanted to hear each student sing. Jennifer's classmates
all said she should go first. She dazzled the teacher. She
also dazzled one young boy who had never heard her
sing before—Walter Williams III.

Williams became Jennifer's number one fan and
decided he wanted to help her become a star. By the
time she was in high school, he became her official
manager. The two formed a partnership that has
lasted nearly twenty years.

"I fell in love with her voice," Williams told VH1 in 2010. "I wanted the whole world to see what I saw in her. I kept pushing her because I knew she was something special."[1]

Jennifer didn't need much pushing. She had plenty of drive all on her own. At age fourteen, she joined her first singing group. The girls called themselves Final Notice. Even then, Jennifer was tall and busty—a far different image than the other two singers. "Even though I didn't fit the look they were going for, they kept me around because I had the most talent," she later said.

The other girls in the group cared more about fashion than music. They enjoyed shopping for skimpy outfits to wear when they performed. For them, the way they looked was just as important as the way they sounded. Jennifer found this frustrating. She wanted to focus on the music.

Also, Jennifer found shopping for clothes difficult. At 5 foot 9 inches tall and with ample curves, she wore size 14. Although that is the average size for women across the United States, designers often focus on styles for smaller-sized women. Because of this, the selection of size 14 clothing for her to choose from often was limited. She also felt embarrassed about buying plus-size clothes.

After a while, Jennifer realized that she didn't fit in with the girls in Final Notice. They cared about style. She cared about singing. She decided to move on.

Next, she joined a group called Fate's Cousins with two of her cousins. They chose this name because it reminded them of the popular singing group Destiny's Child, which they admired. Jennifer was actually the smallest member of this group. Although Fate's Cousins focused on singing, they didn't stay together very long.

Jennifer did detour from her singing for a brief time at age sixteen to take an after-school job in a local Burger King. She wanted some steady income to buy clothes. Very quickly, however, she realized the job was not for her. The grill was hot and the manager unpleasant. Soon, she decided to quit. She wanted to focus on her music and on school, where she took pride in being an honor student.

Williams was delighted. He printed business cards saying Jennifer was available for "weddings, funerals, and church functions." She charged $25 per song. As her manager, Williams kept 10 percent of whatever she made.

Neither of them had money to buy the fancy outfits Jennifer needed for some of these performances. Williams paid for her outfits with his credit card.

After Jennifer performed, he would return the clothes for a refund.

Jennifer did all sorts of performances. She sang at a variety of functions. Over time, she found that the best way to make money was by entering talent competitions on weekends. Many of these contests offered good prize money, and she won most of the ones she entered. Jennifer and Williams felt they were beginning to get the hang of making money in show business. Between school and singing, Hudson rarely had a free moment.

Then Jennifer did something unexpected—she went back to work at Burger King. They had a new manager who was much nicer. This time they gave her the job of working the drive-through window. As a singer, Jennifer loved any job involving a microphone. She entertained the customers with songs as they ordered and picked up their meals.

Ironically, Jennifer's fast food job ended up promoting her singing career. It turned out that the store manager also served as promoter for a local nightclub. He invited Hudson to sing a set or two of songs. He offered her $150. That was far more than she earned working at Burger King. She jumped at the chance to perform at the club. Soon, she started appearing regularly. Once again, she quit her Burger King job. Her fast food career had ended.

Jennifer attended the Paul Laurence Dunbar Vocational Career Academy. This public high school boasted several famous alumni, including actor Mr. T and singer Lou Rawls. Jennifer's cousin, Shari Nichols-Sweat, served as the school's music teacher. During Hudson's senior year, she took some students to see Rawls. Jennifer even got to sing for the famous entertainer.

"At such a young age, she was such an advanced singer," Nichols-Sweat later told the *Chicago Tribune*. She sensed that Jennifer was destined to have a special career.

The school's choral teacher Richard Nunley saw Jennifer's talent as well. "She's a great classical singer," he told the *Chicago Sun-Times* in 2006. "She'd always say, 'Mr. Nunley, I'm going to make you proud of me. I'm going to be a famous singer.'"

Jennifer also made an impression on many of her fellow students at Dunbar. In fact, her classmates voted her "most talented" during her senior year. "I sang in the choir," she later told the *Chicago Tribune*. "I have 'superior' ratings from city and state school competitions. I sang opera, classical, you know, everything." She also took pride in making honor roll and having perfect attendance.

Jennifer believed in living a clean life. Many teens around her smoked or drank. Some took drugs.

Jennifer did none of these things. "I've never had a drink of any kind," she stated proudly in 2007. "I don't smoke and I don't do drugs, I never have and I never plan on it."

Soon after she graduated from high school, her father died of cancer. "We knew it was just a part of life," she said in a 2007 interview. "And it's better to see them gone than for them to suffer."

About this time, Hudson started dating James Payton, whom she had known since childhood. She enjoyed the safety and security of spending time with someone familiar who was from her neighborhood. The pair dated for more than seven years.

After high school, Hudson enrolled at Langston University in Oklahoma. She soon grew homesick for her friends and family, though. She missed seeing her boyfriend, too. She returned home after just one semester. Then she took courses at Kennedy-King College, a community college in Chicago. She felt much more comfortable being closer to home. Meanwhile, she kept singing. She sang at weddings, funerals, and nightclubs. Her friend Walter Williams continued to manage her career.

More and more, Hudson began to realize just what a role image played in a show business career. One incident stood out. At age nineteen, Hudson auditioned as a back-up singer for Barry Manilow.

A singing/songwriting icon, Manilow is best known for 1970s ballads such as "Mandy" and "Weekend in New England." Over the years, he has sold more than 80 million records. He is ranked as the top Adult Contemporary chart performer of all time.[2]

Hudson knew that singing with Manilow, even in a back-up role, was a great opportunity. For the audition, she knew she would have to both sing and dance. She felt comfortable singing, but felt unsure about dancing. She also entered the audition at what would be the peak weight of her life—236 pounds.

Still, Hudson felt she had a great audition. She performed the gospel song "Silver and Gold." The entire group of casting people, including Manilow himself, seemed excited about her performance. After she finished, she went out into the hall to wait for the other hopefuls to finish their auditions. She felt sure she would get the job.

Instead, she was sent home. No one told her why she hadn't been selected after such a strong audition. At the time, she could not understand why she didn't get the job. Looking back on the experience, she thought her weight must have been the reason. "It took me years to finally realize that I didn't get the job because of my size," she later said. At the time, she just felt the disappointment of missing the chance to work with a world-renowned singer.

Soon after, however, Hudson got some good career news. She signed a record deal with Righteous Records. It was a small, Chicago-based independent label, but it still represented a great career opportunity. The record company owner, David Johnson, knew of Hudson from her appearances around Chicago. He felt she could become a successful singer. He also believed, however, that she needed to lose weight if she wanted to be a star. He created a contest between her and another singer on the label to see who could lose the most weight. He offered a cash prize to the winner. Hudson worked hard to win the contest. "If you challenge me, I will accept," she said in her autobiography. "And don't expect to win, because I will crush you."

Determined to win, Hudson started exercising every day. She did aerobics and Tae Bo. She jogged and worked out in the gym. For the first time in her life, she began watching what she ate. She gave up fried foods, red meats, pizza, soda, and ice cream. She ate only grilled chicken, brown rice, and broccoli.

Over time, she began to see dramatic results. Hudson lost sixty pounds and went from size 16 to size 10. She always had faith in her talent. Now she felt as though she looked like a star, too.

One of her music teachers at Kennedy-King College, Rufus Hill, asked his students to sing during his class. After hearing Hudson, he brought a theater coach to listen to her sing. The coach invited her to audition for a role in an upcoming musical called *Big River* that would soon open outside Chicago. Hudson landed the part and considers that her first true "professional" singing job.

Rick Boynton, who was then the Marriott Theatre's artistic director, recalled Hudson's audition in a 2006 interview. "She was so unassuming and really understated in terms of personality," he said. "She just came into the room and opened her mouth, and it was something I had never heard. It was incredible. She got the part immediately."

Singer and actress Felicia Fields, who also had a part in *Big River*, was also blown away. She knew right away that Hudson had a remarkable voice. Hudson's role in the play was small. Still, it offered great experience. She played the part for more than a year.

Soon after the show closed, Williams came to Hudson with an interesting proposal. Disney was holding auditions at a local school. They wanted singers to perform on cruise ships. She didn't really want to go to the audition, but Williams convinced her to give it a try. The casting director hired her as soon as she finished her audition. She was about to leave home for several months to sing at sea.

About the same time, *American Idol* held auditions for its second season. Williams suggested she try out. At first, she wasn't interested. The show was just wrapping up its first season. It was not yet the huge hit it is today. However, when she saw Kelly Clarkson win the first competition, she changed her mind. Maybe a talent competition such as this would give her an opportunity to showcase her singing to a national audience.

To audition for *American Idol,* she would have to pass up the cruise position and give up her record deal. People who already have record contracts are not allowed to compete on *Idol.* The cruise job was a sure thing. So was the record deal. *American Idol,* on the other hand, would be a big risk. She decided to stick with her plans of performing on the cruise ship. She passed on auditioning for the television show.

Hudson had to move to Orlando, Florida, for the Disney job. After two months of rehearsals and training, she left for six months at sea. She played a muse named Calliope in a production of *Hercules: A Muse-ical Comedy.* She also performed a solo of "The Circle of Life" from *The Lion King* in Disney Dreams, a collection of songs and clips from favorite Disney movies.

Hudson enjoyed performing every night, and she loved to hear the reaction of the audience. She soon grew tired of life aboard the ship, however. With eleven decks and measuring more than the length of three football fields, the *Disney Wonder* cruise ship seems like a glamorous place to be. For the 2,500 or so guests who sail on each voyage, it no doubt is a place of wonder. For the 950 cast and crew members, however, it's a job. After a few weeks, traveling the same routes and stopping at the same ports grew boring.

Hudson missed her family, too. She had always been close to her mother and siblings. Being away from them for such an extended period made her homesick. She soon realized that performing on a cruise ship was not something she wanted to do long term. "Two days into my contract I began counting down the days until I could get off the ship and go home," she recalled.

Still, Hudson recognized the value of the job. She later recalled that her time aboard the ship prepared her well for what was about to come. "If I can get through the ship, that means I'm cut out for *Idol*," she later told the *Minneapolis Star Tribune*.

The Disney job also allowed Hudson to save money. With lodging and food covered, she could save most of the money that she earned. That was important since she returned to Chicago with no clear idea of what would come next. She knew she wanted a career as a singer. She just didn't know quite how to make that happen.

As it turned out, Williams did. He had bought airplane tickets to Atlanta so that Hudson could audition for season three of *American Idol*. After just two days back in Chicago, the two flew south for Hudson's next big adventure. Neither of them could possibly imagine just what an adventure it would be.

Chapter 4

"An Idol Tale"

L ike 12,000 other *American Idol* hopefuls, Hudson clutched her numbered bracelet and waited for her number to be called. The show's producers warned no one to leave. If hopefuls weren't there when their number was called, they would miss their chance. Hudson's number was 34403. She hoped it would be a lucky number.

Idol's famous television judges, singer and dancer Paula Abdul, sharp-tongued music mogul Simon Cowell, and bass guitarist and record producer Randy Jackson, weren't part of this early judging process.

Instead, contestants were herded to one of three tables in an area the size of a football field. There, they tried to impress the show's representatives enough to make it to the next round of auditions. Those contestants who passed were sent to the right. Those who were being sent home went to the left.

A day passed. Many in the crowd spent the night on the floor of the Georgia Dome, huddled in sleeping bags. But Hudson wanted to be fresh when her number was called. She and Walter Williams snuck away and slept at a nearby hotel.

Hudson's audition took place early on the morning of the second day. Clad in black corduroy pants and white halter top, she had her hair done up to be really big. She wanted not only her voice, but also her looks, to make an impression on the judges.

As she prepared to sing, other auditions were taking place at the other tables. Hudson needed all her concentration to focus on her own song. "If you don't have a good ear, you're going to be all over the place," she later told VH1. She forced herself to block out all other distractions.

For her audition number, Hudson sang "This Empty Place" by Cissy Houston. Then the producers asked her to sing something more current. She chose Celine Dion's "The Power of Love." They asked her to sing yet a third song. This time she did "Survivor" by

Destiny's Child. After hearing three full songs, the judges sent her to the right. She was safe.

Moving on to the next round meant going back to Atlanta a few weeks later. This time she sang for the show's executive producers. Hudson later recalled that she felt intimidated at meeting these powerful people. Still, she managed to belt out a moving rendition of "The Power of Love." She could see by their reactions that she was going to move forward.

The third round of auditions was held in Pasadena, California. Hudson brought her mother, sister, and Williams along with her for support. This time, Hudson would sing in front of Abdul, Cowell, and Jackson. This performance would determine whether or not she made it onto *American Idol*.

Once again, Hudson wanted to make an impression with her appearance, beginning with her trademark "big hair." For her outfit, she selected a black Versace dress with a hole cut out, exposing her midriff. She thought she looked great. The network censors disagreed. They apparently found the outfit too revealing. When her audition later aired on television, the cutout was colored in. It looked as though she was wearing a plain black dress. She also wore a small sign bearing her contestant number: 34403.

Hudson walked confidently into the audition room. Her fierce determination overcame her nerves.

Randy Jackson noted that she was from Chicago, Illinois, and had just finished working on a Disney cruise ship. "We're going to expect something better than a cruise ship performance, right?" he asked.

"Definitely!" Hudson replied.

"You think you're the next American Idol," Jackson continued. "You're the best that we can find in America?" "Yes," she responded both times.

With that, Hudson launched into her rendition of "Share Your Love With Me" by Aretha Franklin. Less than a minute into the performance, Jackson held up his hand for her to stop. "Brilliant. Absolutely brilliant. The best singer I've heard so far. Brilliant."

Paula Abdul said, "No doubt about it. You can sing your behind off."

Simon Cowell simply said, "Very good. See you in Hollywood."

Hudson emerged from the audition with her golden ticket held high, singing, "I'm going to Hollywood!" Her family and friends hugged her and cheered. "Now that's how you celebrate," Ryan Seacrest said.[1]

Hudson beat steep odds to make it to the Hollywood round of *American Idol*. For season three, more than 80,000 attended auditions in six cities. A total of 117 made it to the first Hollywood round. This means just one out of every 683 contestants made it that far. Over the next week, the number was cut to thirty-two semifinalists and then to twelve finalists.

In early 2004, Hudson traveled to California as one of those 117 hopefuls. Her trip might be as short as a week if she didn't make it into the top 12. It might last as long as three months if she made it to the show's finale. Her goal, she said, was for acid-tongued Cowell, who was known for his sharp criticism of contestants, to tell her she was the best singer he had seen. "I always set goals for myself so I have something to work toward," she later said in her autobiography. "This was my goal for *American Idol.*"

Her *American Idol* experience almost ended early. She made it into the top 32 but not into the top 12. Her performance of John Lennon's classic song "Imagine" was solid, but the judges thought other performers had been even stronger. She thought her *Idol* dream was over.

Then Hudson got an unexpected second chance. She was among eight contestants brought back to try for a "wild card" spot on the show. Four of the eight would earn a spot among the final 12. Hudson sang Whitney Houston's song "I Believe in You and Me." Jackson called it the best performance of the night. He named her as his wild card selection to move forward.

Hudson realized that reaching the top 12 in *American Idol* gave her an opportunity to sing for millions of people each week for as long as she remained in the competition. She resolved to make the most of it.

The competition was exciting . . . and grueling. The final 12 contestants lived together in a large house in the Hollywood Hills. The girls shared a huge bedroom, kind of like a "slumber party," Hudson later recalled.

However, unlike a fun slumber party, the *Idol* experience was hard work. The days were packed full of rehearsals, appearances, and more rehearsals. The tension of preparing to sing a new song on national television each week was grueling. Contestants received their song each Sunday and then had to be ready to perform it live on Tuesday. Each contestant tried to work out arrangements that would showcase his or her unique vocal talents. "Being on *American Idol* was like being on a roller coaster," she later told VH1. "You never knew what was about to hit you."

On Tuesday evening, each of the contestants performed. When the show ended, viewers called or texted to vote for their favorite performer. The window for voting lasted just two hours. The three contestants with the fewest fan votes got pulled aside the next day, and the one with the lowest vote total was sent home.

Hudson's *American Idol* experience had many ups and downs. In the first and third weeks, she placed in the bottom two, facing possible elimination. During the week that featured soul songs, Cowell said she oversang "Baby I Love You" by Aretha Franklin. This meant she tried to make her voice too powerful and ended up off key. Each time, though, she survived. Ironically, the weeks she struggled featured soul and Motown songs. Those were areas that suited her vocal style well.

Hudson got safely through the country music week and movie soundtrack week. She even ended up as the top vote getter during the week that Elton John served as the guest judge.

While on *American Idol*, Hudson realized what it meant to be plus sized in Hollywood. First, one of the musical directors from *Idol* told her early during the competition that everything about her was too big—her voice, her size, her personality. Hudson found this confusing. "Isn't that what being a star is?" she countered. "Stars are larger than life!"

Another time, an interviewer at a red carpet event asked what it felt like to be plus sized. At first, Hudson didn't realize the question was directed at her. Being a size 16 was normal in Chicago. It took her a while to realize the premium that show business places on being slender.

In the early rounds, Cowell constantly criticized her wardrobe choices. He described a conservative white skirt suit as a "leather nurse look." When she wore a metallic silver jumpsuit, he said she looked like "something a Thanksgiving turkey should be wrapped in." He called her custom-made pink taffeta dress "hideous." When she made the final 12, she had access to a stylist and make-up artist. They worked on her "look."

But the most important thing about the show is singing. Week after week, Hudson continued to improve. Her family was in the front row every week cheering for her. Hudson enjoyed having them there to share this special experience.

Each week on *American Idol* revolves around a specific theme. For the first time on season three, *Idol* also brought in guest judges to work with the singers. World-renowned rock star Elton John served as the guest judge during "Top 9" week. He loved Hudson's voice and during rehearsals said he thought she could be the next *American Idol*. She chose to sing his song "The Circle of Life" that week. She had sung it many times while working on the cruise ship.

But he guided her to a new interpretation. Her voice soared through a powerful performance. At the end, the crowd rose and cheered, led by her mother.

That week she was the top vote getter in the entire competition. She was flying high.

The following week revolved around songs from movies, and noted producer/director Quentin Tarantino served as the guest judge. His movies include *Pulp Fiction* and the *Kill Bill* films. Before they met him, the contestants attended a screening of his latest movie, *Kill Bill: Vol. 2*. Hudson was so tired that she fell asleep during the movie. Worse yet, she bumped into Tarantino at the party that followed. Not recognizing him, she mentioned that she had dozed off during the film. When she realized who she was talking to, she hoped he thought she was kidding. But he loved her performance that week of Whitney Houston's "I Have Nothing."

During "Top 7" week, singer/songwriter Barry Manilow served as the guest judge. Hudson was pleased that he remembered her from her audition for him several years earlier. She decided to sing his classic song "Weekend in New England." She worked with him to create what she hoped would be a memorable rendition.

Dressed simply in black pants, a white jacket, and a scarf, she delivered a performance that brought the studio audience to its feet cheering. The judges, too, praised her. Jackson said, "Wow! Yo, Yo! Jennifer, you just get better every week." Cowell, meanwhile, commented that she was part of creating something the show had never had before: "The Battle of the Divas." He was referring to Hudson, Barrino, and London. All three had big voices and big personalities.

Manilow himself offered even higher praise. He said, "In my catalog of songs, it really requires that you have range. I could really not do what Jennifer is doing. It goes to another place."

With feedback like that, Hudson felt confident that she had nailed the song. She thought she was safe for another week. The matter rested in the hands of the voters, though. Both she—and America—were in for a surprise.

Elimination night found her in the bottom group, along with Fantasia Barrino and La Toya London. Ironically, the "Three Divas," who many felt were the strongest singers in the entire competition, were the three lowest vote getters. In the end, it all came down to Hudson and Barrino.

On April 21, 2004, the two singers stood side by side. They held hands as they waited for Seacrest to announce which of them was safe and which was going home. Secretly, Hudson prayed she would be the one voted off. "I was ready," she later wrote in her autobiography. "I knew that *American Idol* was a fantastic launching pad. I didn't care if I won or not. As far as I was concerned, my dream had already come true when I was allowed to sing for millions of Americans for those six incredible weeks." So, it was with mixed emotions that she learned that her *American Idol* experience had ended.

Her fellow contestants were in shock. George Huff buried his face in his hands. Many thought Hudson had a good chance to win the competition. Still, they knew she would come out all right. "I think all of us knew in our hearts when we were looking at Jennifer we were looking at a star," Huff later told VH1.

That week's vote created a firestorm of criticism. People couldn't understand how these three talented singers could all have been in the bottom three. Some believed that racism played a role. After all, all three were African Americans. Three of the four who were "safe" were white.

Others thought Hudson had simply fallen victim to something called "vote splitting." Hudson, London, and Barrino were similar in many ways. They were all young African-American women. They all had big voices and vibrant personalities. While they all appealed to wide audiences, they may have held special appeal to a particular segment of *American Idol* voters. Although people may vote multiple times, many only vote once for their favorite. Many viewers may have liked all three women but chose to vote for only one. Their votes may have been split evenly among Hudson, London, and Barrino. This would cause them all to get somewhat lower totals. Meanwhile, some of the other finalists may have appealed to different groups that didn't overlap so much.

Many people spoke out to proclaim Hudson's talent. Elton John, who had worked with the *Idol* contestants a few weeks earlier, said he was really impressed with the three singers, who "happened to be black, young female singers and they all seemed to be landing in the bottom three."

"These three girls would have the talent to be members of the Royal Academy or Juilliard," John told reporters. "They have great voices. The fact that they are constantly in the bottom three, and I don't want to set myself up here, I find it incredibly racist."[2]

Ryan Seacrest even chastised viewers after announcing Hudson's departure. "You cannot let talent like this slip through the cracks," he said. He urged viewers to make sure they took the time to vote for their favorite singers each week.

Some of Hudson's fans may not have been able to vote for her that week. On the night of the voting, violent storms blew through Hudson's hometown of Chicago. A few tornados even touched down. Thousands of families, including her own, lost power. Not all of them had cell phones. The vote that Hudson lost was described as incredibly close. Could the power outage in Chicago have made the difference?

Newspaper and television reporters tried to stoke the controversy. Hudson refused to be drawn into the drama. "It's a waste of thoughts to even think about what happened," she told *People* magazine.

A report on the *Early Show* on CBS even asked Hudson if she felt she had been "robbed" of her chance to win the *American Idol* crown. Again, Hudson refused to take the bait. "I feel like it was meant to be," she said. "I honestly feel like it's for the better. I feel like I've been blessed."

A few weeks later, Barrino won *American Idol* and secured a recording contract. Hudson, meanwhile, went back to Chicago, wondering what might come next. She hoped that the exposure she had gained on *American Idol* would somehow lead to new career opportunities. Not even in her wildest dreams could she have imagined how exciting those opportunities would be.

Chapter 5

DREAM ROLE IN *DREAMGIRLS*

H udson barely had time to catch her breath from competing on *American Idol* before beginning a singing tour with—*American Idol*. The top ten finishers performed nearly fifty concerts across the United States and into Canada during August and September 2004. After the tension of competing against her fellow *Idol* contestants only months earlier, Hudson loved performing with them. "Being on that tour was like a dream come true because we could finally be successful together," she later recalled in her autobiography.

When the *Idol* tour ended, Walter Williams booked Hudson to perform in nightclubs. She also appeared on Broadway in a one-night performance of the musical *Hair*. At age twenty-two, she had competed on national television. Now she had completed a major tour and was establishing a solo career. She had appeared on Broadway. She felt very successful. As it turned out, she was just getting started.

Six months after finishing *American Idol*, Ed Whitlow approached Hudson. He had been one of the directors on the Disney cruise ship. He asked about working with her to record an album. She moved to Orlando, Florida, and began working on songs in a studio. Meanwhile, they worked to get a record deal in place.

She focused on songs for the album, taking time here and there to do a few performances. She also flew to Los Angeles to audition for a part in the movie version of the Broadway play *Rent*. She didn't get the part, but she wasn't too concerned. She sensed that something else would come along.

In spring 2005, Hudson heard a rumor that she was being considered to play Effie White in a movie adaptation of the Broadway musical *Dreamgirls*. She didn't know about the character, the music, or the play itself. She only knew that Jennifer Holliday had played the role of Effie White on Broadway. She began to learn all about *Dreamgirls*.

Set in the 1960s and 1970s, *Dreamgirls* follows three young women from Chicago who form a singing group called the Dreamettes. As the movie opens, they enter a singing competition. Although they don't win, they draw the notice of a manager, Curtis Taylor, Jr., who offers to help build their career.

The girls become backup singers to a popular rhythm and blues star, James "Thunder" Early. To make Early and the Dreamettes more popular, Taylor changes their sound from rhythm and blues to pop. Eventually, he works to make the girls stars on their own. Renaming the group the Dreams, Taylor also decides to change their image. Effie has been the group's lead singer. As a full-figured woman, she doesn't fit the group's new look, though. He sets up another group member, the slender and beautiful Deena, as the new lead singer.

The story draws much of its power from Effie's anguish. First, she loses her place as lead singer in the group. Eventually, she is replaced altogether. She watches as Deena and the Dreams go on to become superstars. Meanwhile, her career—and her life—fall apart. Gradually, however, she begins a successful solo career. Eventually, she reconciles with her old friends. She even performs with them in their farewell concert as they are breaking up.

The story claims to be fictional. Still, people saw many similarities between the Dreams and the Supremes, a popular group from the 1960s. Both groups changed their names and their images, and both replaced their lead singers with another group member they felt better fit the image they were trying to establish. In both cases, the rejected singers went through a downward career spiral.

The story differed in that Effie managed to pull her life and her career together. Florence Ballard, the former lead singer of the Supremes, did not fare as well. She spent time on welfare after a mostly unsuccessful solo career. She died of a heart attack at the age of thirty-two.

Hudson immediately felt a kinship with the character of Effie. Like Effie, she felt that her weight had cost her some important opportunities. Like Effie, she knew the pain of having appearance count more than talent. "This was practically my life," Hudson said in her autobiography. "This was a role I had to play."

In April 2005, the producers of *Dreamgirls* asked her to fly to New York to audition. She recalls little about the actual audition other than she sang "Easy to Be Hard" from the Broadway musical *Hair*, and she felt it went well. At the end, the producers told her that if she hadn't heard from them by July it probably meant that she hadn't gotten the part.

As it turned out, the casting process took the full three months. More than 780 other women also tried out for the part. The other potential Effies included Fantasia Barrino. She was the woman who had barely beaten out Hudson in the fateful *American Idol* vote when Hudson was sent home. Barrino had gone on to win the competition.

After the audition, Hudson returned to Florida. She tried to go about her business. She kept busy on other projects. Still, she couldn't get Effie out of her mind. She felt a remarkable connection to the character.

Finally, on the last day of July, she got a call. She later recalled how she felt before that call came. "One of those moments when I was down and out, that's when I picked up the phone and they called me," she said in an interview for *Stars* on Broadband TV in 2008. "It always rains before the sun comes out, and then a rainbow comes. Just hold on a little while longer, because dreams can and they do come true."

The producers wanted her to fly to Los Angeles for a second audition. This time they wanted her to sing "And I Am Telling You I'm Not Going." This is the show-stopping song that Effie sings at a dramatic moment in the movie.

When the casting department sent the sheet music for the song, they only sent part of it. Hudson assumed that was all she had to sing. She practiced singing that part for hours. At the audition, however, Hudson heard the woman before her sing the whole song. She realized they expected her to do the same. But she only knew the part she had been sent. She sang that part and left, dejected. She thought she had lost her chance to play Effie.

About a month later, though, the producers called Hudson. They signed her to a two-week hold contract. During this time, she could not sign up to do another job. This contract still did not guarantee her the part, though. It simply gave the producers two more weeks to make a decision. Hudson waited anxiously. "I was on pins and needles the whole time," she later recalled. "I was so close . . . and yet I still felt so far."

At the end of the two weeks, the producers still hadn't made up their minds. They asked her to fly to Los Angeles for a screen test. They told her to pack enough things to stay . . . if she got the role.

She practiced the song "And I Am Telling You I'm Not Going" during the entire six-hour flight. The next day, she did a grueling six-hour screen test. They dressed her like Effie. They did her hair like Effie. They shot dozens of photos. Then she sang the song several times. At the end, they sent her home.

They hadn't hired her. But they hadn't hired anyone else, either. She didn't know what to think.

Back in Orlando, Hudson went into the recording studio the next day. She thought that was the best way to keep her mind off the movie. Within hours, she received a call from the film's director, Bill Condon. He told her she had the role. She boarded a plane that same day and flew back to Los Angeles. She was Effie White!

Ironically, the script called for Effie to be heavier than Hudson. For years, people had told her she needed to lose weight if she wanted to become famous. Now the producers of her first feature film were telling her she needed to gain weight. What a crazy world! Hudson was happy to oblige. She would do anything necessary to make this role work. And she knew how to gain weight. She immediately started a diet of sweets.

Filming began in January 2006. Prior to *Dreamgirls*, Hudson had no formal acting experience. She joined an all-star cast that included Eddie Murphy, Danny Glover, and Oscar-winner Jamie Foxx. Playing Dreamgirl Deena was superstar singer Beyoncé Knowles.

Hudson was nervous at first, especially when one of her first scenes called for her to kiss Foxx, who plays Effie's manager and boyfriend, Curtis Taylor, Jr.

She didn't let being with such big stars intimidate her, though. She knew she had a job to do. "I was so focused, and I wanted it so badly that I really didn't think about it," she later told talk-show host Oprah Winfrey.

Director Condon had taken a huge risk. Casting an unknown actor in a big role for a major film can backfire. Sometimes the spark that showed in the screen test doesn't carry over for a full performance. Condon trusted his judgment, though.

"I have never worked with anyone in my entire career with as much raw talent and openness as Jennifer," Condon told *Vogue* magazine in 2007. "She came to the project with such confidence. She said, 'It may take me a while, but I'll get it.' She had never acted or danced before, and she got it. And it all sprang from her knowing who she is."[1]

Hudson worked hard to "become" Effie. She ate the high-calorie food that Effie ate. She listened to 1960s music. "I felt like I was Effie," Hudson told the *Washington Post*. "Jennifer was nowhere in sight."

Over time, Hudson grew more comfortable in her role. For one thing, she really did identify with her character. At first, Condon had one big concern with Hudson as an actress. She was simply too nice! In the script, Effie was self-centered and had a big ego. She was a true diva. Hudson treated everyone politely and tried to stay in the background. That just didn't work for this role. Condon put Hudson through a series of "Diva 101" lessons to sharpen her personality.

Hudson later told *USA Today* that Condon instructed her to believe "it's all about you. Nothing starts until Effie walks in, and everything ends when she leaves. And you bring it, you bring it. Effie brings everything." Taking that advice, Hudson gradually made the Effie character her own.

Finally, the time came for the scene where she sang "And I Am Telling You I'm Not Going." Condon purposely put off the filming of this climactic scene until the movie was nearly done shooting. He wanted Hudson to gain experience and confidence. The whole movie stands or falls on this performance. Furthermore, Hudson had to compete with the legendary Broadway performance of the song by Jennifer Holliday.

Over and over, they shot the scene. Over and over, Hudson sang the song. Condon issued just one command: no crying. "It's important for the audience to be moved by this character, but not you," he told *USA Today*. "Among all of Effie's qualities, self-pity is not one."

Finally, at the end of the second day, Hudson nailed the song just as Condon wanted it. At that point, the director announced, "Ladies and gentlemen, the star of tomorrow, Ms. Jennifer Hudson."

Hudson's performance perfectly captures Effie's emotional turmoil as she faces the breakup with her longtime boyfriend. The completion of that scene also marked a turning point in her acting career. From that day forward, Hudson felt more confident as an actress. She believed she had earned the respect of her fellow actors as well. "I felt a real shift in the way I was perceived on the set," she later recalled.

When the filming was done and the recording of the soundtrack had been completed, Hudson and the others waited anxiously to see what would happen. They thought they had completed an extraordinary movie. Still, they didn't know what critics and audiences would think.

The finished movie first aired at the Cannes International Film Festival in France in May. This renowned movie event draws directors and stars from all over the world. Many top movies are previewed there. Hudson was invited to go and speak about *Dreamgirls*. She couldn't believe how warmly the audiences reacted to the movie and to her. She felt like a true star. Even more incredible, people were saying she might win an Academy Award for her performance in her very first movie.

At Cannes, Hudson met a Hollywood agent who was impressed by her singing. The agent offered to make a connection with legendary music producer Clive Davis. Davis has played a part in the careers of numerous music superstars, including Rod Stewart, Christina Aguilera, Harry Connick, Jr., Whitney Houston, and season one *American Idol* winner Kelly Clarkson.

In November 2006, Davis bought out Hudson's existing recording contract and signed her to Arista Records. Hudson proudly announced her record deal during an appearance on the *Oprah Winfrey Show*. She said she planned to start recording her first album early in 2007.

Dreamgirls played in three cities in mid-December 2006 and opened nationwide on Christmas Day. The stars waited on pins and needles to see the reaction of the critics and the public. The producers waited anxiously, too. *Dreamgirls* cost $80 million to make, the most expensive film ever made featuring an all African-American cast. Would the film catch fire and earn a profit?

They need not have worried. At the New York City premiere, fans rose in a standing ovation—a rare event at a movie—after Hudson sang "And I Am Telling You I'm Not Going." Hudson said she had dreamed about having such a reception to the song.

As one of the Dreamgirls, it seemed appropriate that her dream would come true.

"It takes your head off," Foxx told *USA Today* when asked about the song. "She does a fantastic job with the acting and then, all of a sudden, she's singing that song. It's beautiful. It was hard not to cry and double up with emotions."

Critics and peers praised both Hudson's singing and acting. Critic Owen Gleiberman of *Entertainment Weekly* called her performance of "And I Am Telling You I'm Not Going" "as grandly shattering a piece of musical acting as the movies have seen since Judy Garland wailed about 'The Man That Got Away' in 1954's *A Star Is Born*."

Claudia Puig of *USA Today* put it this way: "When she's on the screen, the movie shines. When she's not, the whole endeavor suffers."

Rolling Stone critic Peter Travers said, "Hudson's film debut is a glorious, Oscar-ready cause for celebration. She can act. She can nail a laugh with the sassy curl of her lip. She can break your heart by letting her eyes show how she hurts. And she can sing until the roof comes off the multiplex."

Costar Beyoncé Knowles praised Hudson as well. "She gave you chills and made you want to cry," Knowles told *USA Today*. "We were all scared together and we all learned together, and I feel like a big sister when I watch her. I see that people know she is a star."

Oprah Winfrey proclaimed Hudson's performance "a religious experience." Winfrey added, "She makes the little hairs on the back of your neck stand up."

Hudson's favorite praise, however, came from former critic and *American Idol* judge Simon Cowell, who appeared on tape during that same *Oprah Winfrey Show*. After frequently criticizing her on *American Idol*, he had nothing but kind words now. "There are good performances and occasionally there are extraordinary performances. That was extra-ordinary, Jennifer, and I feel very proud for you. I feel we had a very small part in what's happened in your life, and please thank me when you get your Oscar."[2]

Hudson took all the praise in stride. "All I wanted to do was to be part of the movie and not disappoint," Hudson said. "I feel honored—and, like, wow. It was last year at almost this time that I was cast. But to go from that to all of this? I never dreamed this up. That I missed."

Reviews of the overall movie were mostly positive. *Rolling Stone* rated it three and a half stars out of four. *Entertainment Weekly*, on the other hand, only gave it a C–. The movie packed in audiences. The all-star cast helped draw crowds at first. As news spread of Hudson's powerful performance, however, many people came to see her. The movie earned more than $100 million in the United States and another $50 million around the world.

Meanwhile, the soundtrack album for the movie also climbed the charts, peaking at number one on the *Billboard* 200 in January 2007. "Listen" was the first single released from the movie. Then came "And I Am Telling You I'm Not Going."

Dreamgirls racked up many honors as the movie awards season began in early 2007. Hudson won "supporting actress" awards from several noted groups, including the Screen Actors Guild, the National Society of Film Critics, and the National Association for the Advancement of Colored People (NAACP).

Awards season ends with the presentation of the Academy Awards. *Dreamgirls* was nominated for eight awards, including Best Supporting Actor and Best Supporting Actress for Murphy and Hudson. Hudson's competitors for the award were Adriana Barraza, past winner Cate Blanchett, ten-year-old Abigail Breslin, and Rinko Kikuchi.

On February 25, 2007, Hudson sat nervously in the Kodak Theatre in Hollywood waiting for her category to be called. Sitting next to her was Hudson's escort for the evening, director Bill Condon. Academy Award-winning actor George Clooney announced the award winner. When he called her name, she froze for an instant, looking stunned. Then it sank in that she had won.

Clad in a simple brown gown, she tearfully accepted the award. "I cannot believe this," she said. "If my grandmother was here to see me now. She was my biggest inspiration."

That night, a Dreamgirl from Chicago proved that dreams do come true. She had even earned a real Hollywood nickname: J-Hud.

With an Academy Award to her credit and a major recording contract in hand, Hudson seemed destined to make even more dreams happen in the years ahead. Even her wildest dreams, however, could not have prepared her for the intense joys and sorrows she would experience.

Chapter 6

HEARTBREAK
AND HOPE

F ollowing the success of *Dreamgirls*, Hudson's career soared. In March 2007, she became the first African-American singer to appear on the cover of *Vogue* magazine. Soon after that she became the face of Avon's Imari fragrance. Chicago Mayor Richard M. Daley even proclaimed March 6 as "Jennifer Hudson Day." The crowd went wild when their hometown hero spoke and sang a snippet from *Dreamgirls*.

As she grew more and more famous, people asked how she managed to remain grounded. "My faith in

God and my family," Hudson told *Vogue* magazine. "They're very realistic and very normal. They're not into the whole limelight kind of thing, so when I go home to Chicago that's just another place that's home. I stand in line with everybody else, or, when I go home to my mom I'm just Jennifer, (so she says), 'You get up and you take care of your own stuff.' And I love that; I don't like when people tell you everything you want to hear, I want to hear the truth. . . ."

Hudson was soon overwhelmed by offers for movies and other projects. On the set of *Dreamgirls*, costar Beyoncé Knowles had told her that this might happen. Knowles warned her to choose carefully and not take just any role or project that came along.

Hudson took those words to heart. In fact, she turned down a role in the movie *Precious* because it would have required gaining a lot of weight. She knew the role was strong. She thought the movie could be a big hit. Still, she did not want to get locked into roles that revolved around her size. In the end, the role went to newcomer Gabourey Sidibe. Like Hudson, Sidibe earned an Oscar nomination in her first film role, although she did not win. Despite the film's success, Hudson never regretted not taking the part. Following her dream required taking on roles that appealed to her.

She did accept roles in three movies in 2007. The most commercially successful was *Sex and the City*, a movie version of the popular television series about the lives of four single women in New York City. The movie filmed in late 2007 and came out in May 2008. Hudson had the role of Louise, the assistant to lead character Carrie Bradshaw, played by Sarah Jessica Parker. Hudson not only acted in the movie but also recorded a new song titled "All Dressed in Love."

Hudson said she enjoyed taking on a comedy role. She also found it amusing shooting in New York City and having fans come up to greet her. "My first day of shooting, we were in the subway with real New Yorkers—it shocked the mess out of me," she told *Entertainment Weekly*. "They're coming over to Jennifer Hudson and I'm Louise. I'm like, I want to be Jennifer right now, but I'm in the middle of a scene."

Many critics panned the movie, calling it light-weight and overlong. Audiences loved it, though. The film earned more than $400 million worldwide, making it the top-grossing romantic comedy of 2008. The soundtrack album did well, too. It debuted at number 2 on *Billboard*'s list. In a *People* magazine article, Parker praised Hudson's acting, calling her "steady and womanly and gorgeous."

Some people noted that Hudson played the only major African-American character in the movie.

The television show, too, had mostly featured white people. "I'm glad to know that an African-American character was added and I got to be that character," Hudson told *Entertainment Weekly* in a 2008 interview. "I think we all can relate to the show, [and] this makes it so we all can relate even more. And also you're looking at these grown women going through these things, but there's someone younger that's going through these things too, so I kinda covered two bases as a younger character and an African-American character. I killed two birds with one stone!"[1]

Hudson's other big movie gave her a meaty, dramatic role to tackle. Based on a best-selling novel, *The Secret Life of Bees* told the story of fourteen-year-old Lily Owens, who is haunted by the memory of her late mother. Popular young actress Dakota Fanning plays the lead character. Hudson plays the family's maid, Rosaleen, who served as a friend and mother figure to Lily.

Fleeing her abusive father, Lily travels to South Carolina with Rosaleen in search of information about her mother's past. There, the two are taken in by the Boatwright sisters, who work as beekeepers. The film also stars other notables, such as Queen Latifah and Alicia Keys.

Released October 17, 2008, *The Secret Life of Bees* received good reviews and grossed over $37 million.

It also earned several award nominations for its stars. Hudson was nominated for a Black Reel Award for her performance but lost to Queen Latifah.

Hudson also had a small role in a third movie called *Winged Creatures.* The movie tells the story of a group of strangers who form a bond after surviving a random shooting at a Los Angeles diner. The movie featured several major stars, including Kate Beckinsale, Dakota Fanning, and Forest Whitaker. Hudson plays Whitaker's daughter. Despite the strong cast, the film received mixed but mostly negative reviews. It was later retitled *Fragments* for release on DVD. Hudson did not worry about the movie's lack of success. She realized that just as every song is not a hit, neither is every movie.

In between all her other projects, Hudson kept working on her first album. The project took a long time to develop. She wanted to choose songs that would appeal to her audience while also remaining true to her voice and what she liked to sing. In all, she recorded about sixty songs over a period of nearly two years. Finally, she selected thirteen songs she liked best and thought fit well together.

Meanwhile, Hudson's personal life thrived. About the time she was filming *Sex and the City,* she began to take notice of an actor named David Otunga. Otunga had an interesting background. He held a bachelor of science degree in psychology from the University of Illinois and a law degree from Harvard. Tall and handsome, he also had been a contestant in the TV reality series *I Love New York 2*.

Earlier that year, she had ended her longtime relationship with James Payton. She was now unattached. Soon she and Otunga met. Both felt a strong attraction. Almost immediately, they became a couple. They spent much of the summer of 2008 traveling together as Hudson toured to promote her upcoming album. When she had a show in Boston, he showed her around Harvard, where he had gone to college.

Hudson was thrilled when she was asked to sing the national anthem for the opening of the Democratic National Convention in Denver, Colorado. At the convention, Barack Obama became the first African American nominated to run for president. She felt proud to be part of this historic moment in the nation's history.

Otunga and Hudson's mother accompanied her to Denver. While they were there, Otunga asked her mother for permission to marry Hudson. She gladly gave her blessing. On September 12, 2008, Hudson received a special surprise on her twenty-seventh birthday. Otunga asked her to marry him and presented her with an engagement ring. But they planned not to marry right away.

For one thing, Hudson had a whirlwind schedule around her soon-to-be-released album. Otunga, meanwhile, had plans to pursue his own dream. The man with a law degree from Harvard wanted to become a professional wrestler. He spent the next several months training in Tampa, Florida. In May 2009, he began a successful career with World Wrestling Entertainment. In fact, he is a two-time holder of the WWE Tag Team Championship belt.

Hudson's debut album, titled simply *Jennifer Hudson*, came out on September 27, 2008. A number of well-known artists wrote songs for the album, including Ne-Yo, Timbaland, and Diane Warren. Some singers write their own songs. Others want to concentrate on their singing. While Hudson chose to let others write the songs for the album, she picked the subjects for most of them. "I want my music to have substance and meaning and bring real music back," she told Kevin McKeough of *Chicago Magazine* in 2008. "A lot of music today is bubblegum and pop and mainly about a catchy melody. I sing about things that'll help somebody out."

The album also featured appearances by artists Ludacris, T-Pain, and Hudson's old *American Idol* friend Fantasia Barrino. Despite this all-star lineup, the album drew mixed reviews from the critics. *Entertainment Weekly* gave the debut album a B–. The review said Hudson tried too hard to provide "something for everybody," leading to a hodgepodge of sounds and styles. A *New York Daily News* reviewer also felt that she strayed from her strengths in an attempt to appeal to a younger audience. However, he also offered praise for her performance on several specific tracks.

The album cover also sparked controversy. Some people claimed that the cover photo had been altered to make her look thinner. They thought that sent the wrong message about women's body sizes. In response, Hudson told *Chicago Magazine*, "Who doesn't Photoshop pictures at this point? The album cover is close to my true size. I want to be as real and natural as possible."

Overall, the album was a huge success, debuting at number two on the *Billboard* album charts. It sold more than 200,000 copies the first week and more than half a million copies overall. It also earned four Grammy Award nominations. The Grammy Awards are the highest honor in the recording industry.

The album yielded three singles. The first, "Spotlight," cracked the top 30 on the *Billboard* charts. It peaked at number two on the Rhythm and Blues (R&B) charts.

"I've waited my whole life for this moment," Hudson said in an interview for the CBS *Early Show*. "It's a great mix because I want to be able to have something for everyone on my album."

Hudson felt on top of the world. Her new movie, *The Secret Life of Bees*, was drawing positive reviews. Her debut album stood near the top of the charts. She wore a brand-new engagement ring on her finger. In addition, she had an exciting film role ahead of her. She had been cast to play Winnie Mandela in a film biography of the famous South African politician and activist.

Then tragedy struck. On October 24, Hudson's sister, Julia, returned to the family home in Chicago to find her mother lying on the living room floor. At first, she thought her mother had fallen. Then she saw blood. She ran screaming from the home and frantically called 911.

She struggled to maintain her composure enough to tell the person on the phone what was happening. "My mama, my mama," she moaned. Asked for details by the person at the 911 center, she tried to describe what she saw. At one point during the call, she screamed, "Someone killed my mother! . . . There's a bullet hole in the front door!"

Police rushed to the scene. Not only was Darnell Donerson dead, but Jason Hudson, Jennifer and

Julia's brother, had also been shot to death in his bed. Julia's seven-year-old son, Julian, was missing. Police believed that he had been kidnapped by whoever had committed the murders.

The police learned that a neighbor had heard gunshots around 9:00 A.M. that morning. She hadn't bothered to report it. Gunshots were common in that area of town.

Jennifer Hudson learned of the tragedy in Florida, where she was visiting her fiancé Otunga. She was stunned to learn of the sudden death of her beloved mother and brother. She knew that Englewood had a high crime rate. Still, the Hudson family had lived there for many years. They felt safe in their home.

Jennifer Hudson immediately offered $100,000 for information leading to the safe return of her nephew. "I don't care who you are, just let the baby go," Julia Hudson said the next day as she stood beside Julian's father, Greg King. "I know he's out there. Just let him go."

On her MySpace page, Jennifer Hudson wrote, "Please keep praying for our family that we get Julian King back home safely. If anyone has any information about his whereabouts please contact the authorities."

Three days later, however, Julian's body was found in an SUV parked on the west side of Chicago. The boy had died from multiple gunshot wounds.

Police discovered a handgun in a vacant lot near the abandoned vehicle. They believed the gun had been used to commit all three murders.

Jennifer Hudson had the sad duty of identifying Julian's body at the Chicago city morgue. She asked the spokesperson for the medical examiner's officer to tell the general public to respect the family's privacy during their time of grieving.

Friends and neighbors tried to support the Hudson family. They left a mountain of stuffed animals and flowers in front of the family's home. Because of Hudson's fame, the case drew national publicity as well. Many of Hudson's celebrity friends expressed their condolences.

Even Barack Obama, who was at the time in the final days of his campaign for president, expressed his sympathy. "Michelle [Obama] and I were absolutely heartbroken to learn about this unimaginable tragedy, and we want Jennifer to know that she is in our thoughts and prayers during this very difficult time," he said. Just days later, he was elected as the nation's first African-American president.

Some people wondered why Hudson's mother continued to live in a modest home in a dangerous part of Chicago. Jennifer Hudson had earned millions of dollars from acting and singing. She could have bought her mother a big house almost anywhere.

But Donerson had remained in the family home because she loved it there. She wanted to be close to her friends. She wanted to be close to her church. She felt safe and comfortable in the house she had lived in for so long.

As it turned out, the murders had nothing to do with where she lived. This was no random act of violence. Police immediately zeroed in on a suspect. On the same day the first two bodies were found, police took William Balfour into custody. Balfour was Julia's estranged husband. At first, police held him for parole violations while they continued their investigation. They called him a "person of interest" in the case.

After several years of marriage, Balfour and Julia Hudson had split up the previous winter. They had many arguments after the breakup. In fact, Balfour had come to the Hudson household on the morning of the murders. Julia said he had accused her of ignoring him. She said he flew into a rage because he believed she was seeing another man.

Balfour already had a criminal record. He had previously spent several years in prison. Those charges included attempted murder and vehicular hijacking. After a month-long investigation, police charged Balfour with three counts of murder.

"We're going through this stage where we're just sad and in shock," said Dorothy Hudson, Julia and Jennifer Hudson's aunt. Dorothy Hudson and her husband owned a Chicago funeral home, and they handled the funeral arrangements.

After the murders, Hudson came home to be with her family and support her sister. The funeral took place on November 3, 2008. Instead of flowers, the family asked that donations be given to the newly created Hudson-King Domestic Violence Protection Fund. The family asked for privacy so that they could grieve.

Hudson later recalled the time during an interview for VH1. "It's all a blur," she said. "It was surreal." She added that she stayed in one room for two weeks as family and friends came in and out.

Hudson grieved at the loss of her beloved mother, brother, and nephew. She also felt strange realizing that she could have been killed as well. She later revealed that she had planned to be in Chicago at the time of the murder visiting her family. However, her fiancé invited her to Tampa, Florida, to watch him perform in a WWE event. Instead of flying to Chicago, she flew to Tampa. Had she been in Chicago, she could have been in the house and been a victim, too.

"That's one of the things that saved my life," Hudson said. "I could have been home with my mom then. He wanted me to come out to Florida with him instead of going to Chicago. I flew out to see him; that's why I'm still here."

Hudson withdrew from public life for several months after the murders. She needed to recover from the physical toll of her busy year and the emotional toll of losing her family members to murder.

Hudson also had another reason for temporarily backing away from her career. That fall, she discovered that she was pregnant!

How did she get through the difficult months following the murders? "My family, my baby, and God," she later told Oprah. "And holding on to the things they taught us. The only thing I can do to honor their memory is to make them proud. And that's what keeps me going."[2]

A year that had begun with great joy had ended in great sorrow. Still, Hudson had a baby growing inside of her and new career opportunities ahead.

Heartbreak lay behind her. She believed hope lay ahead.

Chapter 7

ROLE MODEL

J ennifer Hudson stayed out of the spotlight for several months after the murder of her mother, brother, and nephew. She needed time to heal from the shock and trauma of her loss. She also wanted to protect the baby growing insider her. She needed to regain her strength as she prepared to be a mother.

Hudson had been scheduled to begin filming the biography of Winnie Mandela early in 2009. She didn't want to face the rigors of spending months shooting in South Africa while she was pregnant. She did not think that would be healthy for her or the baby. She didn't want people to know yet that she was pregnant, though. She didn't know what to tell the film's producers.

In the end, she simply asked if the filming could be postponed for personal reasons. The producers may have thought she was still recovering from the death of her family members. Delaying a major motion picture project costs money. As the star of the movie, Hudson would be in most of the scenes. Filming could not proceed without her. The delay affected the entire cast and crew. The movie was set to be filmed in South Africa. Changing the filming dates meant changing many arrangements half a world away.

Hudson worried about what might happen. Sometimes if a star isn't available when a movie is ready to shoot, the producers simply give the part to another actor. In some cases, the entire project gets canceled. Much to Hudson's relief, the producers said they would wait. They really wanted her to play the part. They told her to take all the time she needed. Filming would begin when she was ready.

Bit by bit, Hudson's pain began to subside. Gradually, life started to get back to normal. After three months, Hudson began to make public appearances again. She didn't tiptoe back into the spotlight. She exploded back into view with a pair of high-voltage appearances. She chose to do brief performances. She wanted to avoid placing too much strain on her pregnant body.

On February 1, 2009, she made her dramatic return to the stage. That night, she performed the national anthem at Super Bowl XLIII in Tampa, Florida. Millions of fans around the world tuned in. Most were preparing to watch the game, but many wanted to see Hudson perform, too. They realized that it was her first public appearance since her family tragedy.

Wearing a white top with black pants and jacket, Hudson climbed onto the stage. It had been months since she had performed, and she knew that a worldwide audience was watching. "When I stood on the field facing the crowd, there was a roar in the stadium unlike anything I had ever heard," she later recalled. "Luckily, once I started to sing, the tension faded away, as it always does. I sang from my heart and soul that night—and I think it showed."

Her fans certainly agreed. The people in the stadium responded to her performance with a thunderous ovation. Soon after, her cell phone buzzed with a message from actor Jamie Foxx. Her costar from *Dreamgirls* texted, "Amazing. It brought tears to my eyes."

"This was such an important performance, because it's the first time everyone has seen Jennifer [since the tragedy]," said Rickey Minor, who produced the pre-game show. "But she's in such a great place, with such great spirits, and time can heal her wounds. She's on fire right now and totally grounded."

A few days later, the video for her new single, "If This Isn't Love," premiered. Then, on February 8, she performed live at the Grammy Awards. Dressed in a sparkling black dress, she belted out the powerful ballad "You Pulled Me Through" from her album. The theme of pulling through something seemed very appropriate in light of her recent trauma. She delivered a powerful performance. Toward the end, she got choked up. Tears came to her eyes, and she almost whispered the final lyrics. When the song ended, the audience rose to its feet in a standing ovation. J-Hud was back!

Hudson also celebrated winning a Grammy that evening. Her debut album was honored as the year's Best Rhythm and Blues (R&B) Album. Whitney Houston, one of her idols, presented the award. That made it even more special to Hudson. In her moving acceptance speech, Hudson thanked her family members both in heaven and here on earth.

Hudson made time in her busy schedule for an encore wedding proposal. The previous fall, Otunga had proposed on her birthday. She decided to return the favor. On April 7, 2009, his twenty-ninth birthday, she surprised him with a five-carat engagement ring. She had it designed by Neil Lane, who had also designed the ring Otunga had given her. Neither Lane nor Hudson knew Otunga's ring size. The ring that Lane first made was too large, so they had it resized. "They were so lovey-dovey and so sweet to each other," Lane told *People* magazine. "He was very protective of her, and they were so in love."

That spring, Hudson began touring with Robin Thicke. In May, however, she suffered throat fatigue. As a result, she had to reschedule some of her tour dates. She also tried to slow down her schedule as her baby's birth drew near.

She made an exception to perform at the memorial service for music legend Michael Jackson on July 7, 2009. The famed singer had died suddenly of a heart attack on June 25. He died at the age of fifty as he prepared to go on his first tour in more than a decade. His death came less than three weeks before the first concert date.

Like millions of other fans, Hudson had grown up listening to Jackson's music. She was only a year old when he released his *Thriller* album. The best-selling album of all time worldwide, the album earned a record eight Grammy Awards.

Attired in a knee-length white dress, Hudson sang what *MTV.com* writer Eric Ditzian described as a "gospel-tinged version" of Jackson's 1991 hit, "Will You Be There?" Near the end of the emotionally charged performance, a recording of Jackson's voice softly spoke the lyrics as Hudson sang. "We love you Michael," Hudson said as she finished singing.

On August 10, Hudson gave birth to David Daniel Otunga, Jr. "It was love at first sight," Hudson later recalled in her autobiography. "As I held him close, I cried more than my newborn son." Becoming a mother somehow seemed to help as she continued to grieve the loss of her own mother. "My wish is to be at least half as good as my mother was, and as loving as she was," she told *Essence* magazine in 2011.

Motherhood agreed with Hudson. When young David was about six months old, she went on *Good Morning America* to talk about being a parent. "It is the best thing ever," Hudson told host Robin Roberts. "I have the best baby ever." Not only did he give her kisses and go crazy when she sang to him, but he also thought he was a dog. "I have three dogs . . . so he thinks he's one of them," Hudson said. "So when he sees other babies he growls."

Hudson had gained about thirty-five pounds during her pregnancy. That's a fairly normal weight gain. However, she was disappointed to find that even after David's birth, her weight hovered around 235 pounds. This was the most she had weighed in many years. That disturbed her. As soon as she was able, she began a regular walking routine. But even as she was losing the "baby weight" she had gained, she resolved to lose much more.

Hudson met with a team of people from Weight Watchers®. Liz Josefsberg became her Weight Watchers leader. At first, Hudson did not fully buy into the program. She couldn't believe that she could still eat her favorite foods. Josefsberg explained that it was planning and portion size that made the difference. By keeping track of the points that the program assigns to different foods, people can mix and match foods they like and still lose weight.

At first, Hudson tried to create her own version of the Weight Watchers program. She followed some of the guidelines but not all of them. This didn't work. After two weeks, she found that she had actually gained weight. After that, she decided to fully follow the program. She immediately saw results. She became so enthusiastic about Weight Watchers that she signed on to become a spokeswoman for the program.

Hudson coupled her new eating habits with increased exercise. She did a wide range of activities. Some days she biked. Others she played basketball. Sometimes she worked out at the gym. When short of time, as she often was, she did a workout called trilogy, which combines cardio and strength. She did 25 squats, 25 push-ups, and 25 ab moves, and then rested a minute. Then she did them in reverse order and rested another minute. She did this for fifteen minutes.

Soon, she began to see a big difference in how she looked. Even better, she felt healthier and more energetic. Between her frequent singing and television appearances and her appearance in a series of Weight Watchers ads, the world got to watch as Hudson went on her weight-loss journey.

By mid-2010, she had gone from a size 16 to a size 6. People took notice. *Fitness* magazine named Hudson and reality star Kelly Osbourne as the Best Celebrity Bodies of 2010. *InStyle* magazine named her the "Makeover of the Year." While expressing pride in her achievement, Hudson told the magazine, "I don't want to lose any more weight, and you're never going to see me skinny. I think this is a good, natural size for me."

In February 2011, Hudson appeared on the *Oprah Winfrey Show*. She told Oprah that she had lost eighty pounds. "I wanted my body back," she told Oprah. "I always say if you don't like something, change it."

But she said that even more important than the number of pounds was the way she felt. "I look at it by age," she told Oprah. "I feel like I gained 10 years of my life back."

Throughout the rest of 2011, Hudson continued to gain notice for her weight loss. *US* magazine named her one of the most talked about bodies of the year. She continued to do ads for Weight Watchers. One of the ads showed Hudson talking to a former, heavier version of herself.

Hudson has described this as the third major weight loss in her life. She lost about sixty pounds in her early twenties when she was launching her singing career. Then she lost back the weight she had gained for her role in *Dreamgirls.* Both of those times she soon gained back the weight she had lost.

This time, however, Hudson felt confident she could maintain her weight loss. She found the Weight Watchers program easy to follow. She liked how she felt at a lighter weight. She also liked how her fans responded to her new look.

Since becoming a spokesperson for Weight Watchers, Hudson has inspired many other people to begin their own weight-loss journeys. Some seventy-five members of her extended family have also joined the program, losing a total of more than 2,000 pounds. One of her cousins lost an amazing 112 pounds. Hudson even has a Weight Watchers center named after her in Chicago.

Hudson's weight loss has not been without controversy, however. She has received some negative feedback, especially on Twitter. Some of her Twitter followers accused her of using a surgical procedure to lose weight. Hudson strongly denied this claim. She knew her weight loss was the result of hard work and healthy eating.

Then Joy Behar on *The View* quoted Hudson as saying she was now a size zero. This started another flap, as some people felt that was too much weight to lose.

Hudson grew angry over this accusation. She denied ever making such a claim. "I wasn't even on the show," she said in *Ebony* magazine. "I never said I was a size zero. I got crucified by I don't know how many people who cussed me out because they said I'm putting out the wrong message and telling people to be a size zero. . . . I never said that. People say I'm always dwelling on my size. No, I'm not! Everyone else is always dwelling on my size."[1]

"I'm showing people a healthier way," Hudson said. She noted that she had started at a size 16 and lost her weight over two years. "So what's been drastic about that? I don't know much about the surgeries or any of that stuff. If it couldn't be done naturally, it couldn't be something for me. I work hard for every single thing. Just because you didn't see me working doesn't mean I wasn't."

Liz Josefsberg, the leader of Weight Watchers, agreed that Hudson worked hard and lost weight the right way. "People believe losing weight has to be a painful experience when it really doesn't," said Josefsberg. "When you find the right balance, it's enjoyable."

Hudson credits her weight-loss success to a very special source of inspiration—her son, David. "He's like my motivation for everything," she told the *CBS Early Show* in 2011. She wants to be healthy and set a healthy example for her son.

In 2012, new mother Jessica Simpson took over as the spokesperson for Weight Watchers. Hudson offered some advice for her replacement. "Write down what you're eating," she said, "you'll be far more aware. And be active with the baby. Be active with them, and you'll stay in shape. There's no workout like running around after a two-year-old."

Once Hudson felt settled in with baby David, she dove back into her work. In December 2009, ABC aired a Christmas special titled "Jennifer Hudson: I'll Be Home for Christmas." Filmed in Chicago, the special included visits with family, friends, and special places in town.

Several important projects came her way in 2010. In January, a strong earthquake struck Haiti. It caused extensive damage in a country already struggling with extreme poverty. Soon after, Hudson appeared on a telethon to support relief efforts. She performed the classic song "Let It Be" by the Beatles. The telecast raised more than $60 million in donations.

In February, she joined several other artists at the Grammy Awards in a special tribute to Michael Jackson. Soon after that she performed at the White House. There, she joined icons such as Smokey Robinson and Bob Dylan for "A Celebration of Music from the Civil Rights Movement."

Spring of 2010 found Hudson in South Africa to film the movie *Winnie*. The movie had been troubled from the start. At first, Hudson had to delay filming because of her pregnancy. Originally scheduled to shoot in 2009, the movie actually filmed a year later.

Hudson found the project extremely challenging. She hated being away from her family. She missed being with her baby. The long days of shooting in South Africa began to take a toll. She was exhausted and emotionally drained.

The role itself presented many challenges. For one thing, Hudson had to master South African dialect so she would sound authentic. Furthermore, Winnie Mandela is a controversial, larger-than-life figure.

She is revered by many in her native country as an activist and the former wife of Nelson Mandela. Nelson Mandela, played by Terrence Howard in the film, is a Nobel Peace Prize winner and former president of South Africa. Both of the Mandelas played huge roles in ending apartheid, a system of segregation in South Africa.

Some complained about casting American actors to play these South African icons. The Creative Workers Union of South Africa believed that bringing in American actors undercut South Africa's chance to develop its own talent. "It can't happen that we want to develop our own Hollywood and yet bring in imports," union president Mabutho Sithole said.

Winnie Mandela herself expressed concern about the movie. She asked to review the screenplay in 2010 before filming began. The movie's producers refused. At one point, legal action was threatened to keep the movie from proceeding.

"I have absolutely nothing against Jennifer," Mandela said in a 2011 interview with CNN, "but I have everything against the movie itself. I was not consulted. I am still alive. I think that it is total disrespect to come to South Africa, make a movie about my struggle and call that movie some translation of a romantic life of Winnie Mandela. I think it is an insult."

The movie debuted at the Toronto Film Festival in September 2011. Before the event, buzz about the movie was strong. Some thought the film might even earn Hudson a second Oscar nomination. Critics panned the film, however. In his review for *The Hollywood Reporter*, David Rooney said it seemed that both Hudson and Howard were miscast. He added, however, that "her measured performance is one of the strengths" of an otherwise lackluster film.

Writing in *The Guardian*, Ed Gibbs said the movie played "much like a primetime telemovie." After the poor reviews at the festival, the movie went back for further editing.

Beginning in late 2009, Hudson began recording material for her second album. She had tried to include a bit of everything on her first album to appeal to a wide audience. This time she vowed to make it more personal and include songs that meant a lot to her.

She recorded the album in bits and pieces in between her acting roles and other commitments. She worked in studios in Dallas, Miami, Chicago, New York, Hollywood, Santa Monica, and Denver. The album, titled *I Remember Me*, debuted March 22, 2011, at number two on the *Billboard* charts, selling 165,000 copies in its first week. The cover photo showed Hudson looking svelte and confident.

Noted songwriters Alicia Keys, Ne-Yo, and R. Kelly contributed songs to the album. The lead single, "Where You At," written by R. Kelly, reached the top ten on the *Billboard* charts. Other singles from the album included "No One Gonna Love You" and "I Got This."

Ne-Yo told *E! Online* that Hudson was ready to get personal on her second studio album. "She's gone through a lot over the last year, so she has a lot to talk about," he said. "She's definitely gotten stronger. The things that she's gone through and for her to still be upbeat and happy, it's amazing."

"My voice is one of the few things that hasn't dramatically changed in my life," Hudson said in an interview for *Newsweek*. "Ten years ago, I was singing in Chicago theaters and living in my mom's house. That's all vanished. But I hear my voice, and I'm like, 'OK, that's me. That's the same girl I knew way back in high school, who used to drive her music teacher crazy by singing Aretha songs at the top of her lungs.'"

In the title song, Hudson sings about remembering who she used to be. In the lyrics, and in her voice, the listener can sense all she's been through in recent years—both good and bad.

"I named it *I Remember Me* because I feel like in 29 years I have led over four different lives," Hudson said during an interview at the Oscar ceremony in

February 2011. "And the album is helping to remember the old stuff and celebrate the new. It is a disc of everything I've been through. I don't have much from my old stuff to grasp at, so the only way I remember me is from my voice or the scar on my hand. That's a part of me and I want to remember it all, every minute."

"Hudson's unmannered strength and class shine through," wrote Elysa Gardner in a review for *USA Today*. "The warmth in her big, old-school voice bespeaks faith in the future, and it carries the listener along for a good part of the ride," added Caroline Sullivan in a review for *The Guardian*.

In June 2011, Hudson launched a nationwide tour to support her album. That same month, she also signed on to play a nun in the slapstick movie *The Three Stooges*. She took the role to honor her mother, who loved the comedy trio.

Another big project involved completing her autobiography titled *I Got This: How I Changed My Ways and Lost What Weighed Me Down*. The book came out in January 2012. In addition to telling her life story, Hudson focuses on her weight loss. She credits the Weight Watchers program and shares some of her favorite Weight Watchers recipes.

Buoyed by the success of her book, Hudson began 2012 on a high note. Then, like many others, Hudson was stunned and saddened by the sudden death of superstar singer Whitney Houston. Houston died on February 11, 2012, at age forty-eight. Hudson had grown up admiring Houston's powerful voice. In fact, she remembered singing along to "I Will Always Love You" as a youngster. She had always considered Houston one of her idols. Losing her hurt badly.

At the Grammy Awards the next day, Hudson joined others in offering a tribute to the fallen star. She performed a simple, but moving version of "I Will Always Love You." At the end, she altered the lyrics to say, "Whitney, we will always love you."

In the spring of 2012, Hudson had to relive the murder of her mother, brother, and nephew when William Balfour went to trial. Three and a half years after the murders took place, the pain still hung fresh in her heart.

The trial began on April 23 in Chicago. Hudson attended each day in court. Otunga took leave from the WWE so he could be with her. He supported her through the painful process.

In all, prosecutors called more than eighty witnesses. Jennifer Hudson was the first to testify. She choked back tears as she testified that no one in her family wanted Julia to marry Balfour. "We didn't like the way he treated her, and I didn't like the way he treated my nephew," Hudson said.

Later, Julia Hudson testified that Balfour had repeatedly threatened her and her family. Despite that, she had never called police or filed for a protection order. "I didn't believe him," she responded when asked why.

Julia testified that Balfour had shown up at her house early on the day of the murders. The two had argued, as they often did. A neighbor testified that she heard two shots coming from the direction of the Hudson house around 9:00 A.M. that day. She didn't call police because it was fairly common to hear shots in the neighborhood.

On May 11, 2012, the jury found Balfour guilty of murdering Hudson's mother, brother, and seven-year-old nephew. At first, the jury was split 9–3 in favor of conviction. After further discussion and after examining Balfour's cell phone records, jurors reached a unanimous decision. They found Balfour guilty of all charges against him, including three counts of first-degree murder.

Jennifer Hudson sat between her fiancé and her sister and cried silently as the verdict was read. Otunga held her hand. Afterward, the Hudsons offered a statement of thanks to police, prosecutors, and others involved in the trial: "We have felt the love and support from people all over the world and we're very grateful. We want to extend a prayer from the Hudson family to the Balfour family. We have all suffered terrible loss in this tragedy. It is our prayer that the Lord will forgive Mr. Balfour of these heinous acts."

On July 24, Hudson returned to the courthouse for Balfour's sentencing. She and her sister, Julia, sat silently and dabbed at their eyes with tissues. Still proclaiming his innocence, Balfour said, "My deepest sympathies go to Julian King [the seven-year-old stepson who was murdered]. I loved him. I still love him."

Judge Charles Burns called those claims "an insult to all of us." As he imposed a sentence of life in prison with no chance for parole, the judge added, "Your heart is an arctic night, and your soul is as barren as dark space."[2]

Hudson and her family left the courthouse immediately after the sentencing. They had no comment for the media. But the end of the case brought a sense of closure. Now they could try to truly put the tragedy behind them.

After the Balfour trial ended, Hudson launched into a flurry of projects. In May 2012, she signed on for a role in the movie *Lullaby*. This film tells the story of a young man who learns that his estranged father plans to take himself off life support. Hudson plays a nurse.

In the summer of 2012, she also filmed *The Inevitable Defeat of Mister and Pete*. This movie is about two inner-city youth who must fend for themselves for the summer when their mothers are taken away by the authorities. Other stars in the film include Jordin Sparks. Like Hudson, Sparks is a former *American Idol* contestant. She won the competition in 2007. Noted musician Alicia Keys served as an executive producer for the film.

Hudson also took a role in the television show *Smash*. She portrays Veronica Moore, a Broadway star. In addition to acting in *Smash*, Hudson is recording original music for the show. In a promotion for the show, she said she enjoys the challenge of juggling different tasks. "One minute you're in the studio, the next second you're doing choreography, the next second you're acting," she said.

With her busy work schedule, Hudson works hard to maintain family time. While filming *Smash* scenes in New York City during summer 2012, she brought three-year-old son David along to one of the shoots. Photographers shot them holding hands during a break.

Meanwhile, Hudson's long-awaited Winnie Mandela biopic moved toward release. As director Darrell Roodt told the *Toronto Globe and Mail* before the film opened in Canada in October 2012, "The good news about the negative stuff is it gave us time to reconsider the film and tweak it more. The film that's out there now, I'm pretty happy with it." Critics gave the revised movie a better, but still lukewarm, reception the second time around.

While Hudson keeps busy with all her projects, her fiancé has seen his own acting career pick up steam. During the summer of 2012, Otunga signed a movie deal of his own. He was cast in the movie *The Call*, which was released in 2013. The film stars Halle Berry.

Hudson hasn't forgotten about her music. In 2012, she recorded a version of Brahms' Lullaby for Pampers. The diaper maker made the song available for free download on its Web site. As a proud mother herself, Hudson took special joy in this project. "To me it's like a perfect fit to be able to do this and be able to share with other moms at the same time," she said in an interview with AOL's *Boombox*.

To thank Hudson, Pampers donated $100,000 to the Julian D. King Gift Foundation. Julia and Jennifer Hudson started the foundation in memory of Julia's slain son. The foundation provides a variety of supports for youth. For instance, on August 14, 2012, Jennifer and Julia handed out school supplies to five thousand Chicago students. They also run a holiday toy drive for disadvantaged children.

In the AOL *Boombox* interview, Hudson revealed that she was gearing up to start working on her next album. "I plan on writing more and getting more involved," she said. "More creatively, musically, in just every way."

Among all of these projects, Hudson also found time to launch a new clothing line in September 2012. The line features affordable designer clothes for women of all sizes. "I want [my shoppers] to know that my line is for every girl, every woman, every size," Hudson told *InStyle* magazine. "And it doesn't matter how much money you make. I just want to share my passion for fashion with people who have the same passion."

Hudson also recalled her childhood thoughts on fashion. She never thought she needed brand-name clothes or shoes. "With me wearing it, it makes it special by itself," she told *Redbook* magazine. "That's what I grew up saying! And now I have my own line, and I can't believe it."

Meanwhile, her work schedule shows no signs of slowing down. For instance, in December 2012, she traveled to Oslo, Norway. There, she sang at the Nobel Peace Prize Concert.

Hectic work and travel schedules have continued to delay plans for Hudson and Otunga to marry. They have been engaged for several years now. Like most brides, Hudson knows what she wants her wedding to look like. And she wants it to take place in Chicago. Rich and famous, she could live anywhere. She chooses to remain in her hometown. At this point, she knows the who, what, and where for her wedding. She just needs to finalize when.

The long delay led to rumors that her relationship with Otunga was crumbling. Some people reported he was getting tired of waiting to get married. The couple tried to put those rumors to rest. In September 2012, both Otunga and Hudson appeared on *Oprah's Next Chapter*. There, Hudson revealed that she hoped to soon add another member to their family. "That is the next part of my dream," she said. "I really want a little girl." Both fiancé David and son David also have said they want to add a baby girl to the family.

Hudson announced in the December 2012 issue of *Redbook* that wedding plans with big David are under way. She said she is keeping the exact plans secret in hopes of maintaining some privacy.

Who knows what lies ahead for this talented singer and actress? From modest beginnings, Hudson has risen to worldwide fame. In 2013, she even got a star on the Hollywood Walk of Fame, and she sang "America the Beautiful" at Super Bowl XLVII in New Orleans, Louisiana, with the choir from Sandy Hook Elementary School.

What keeps Hudson grounded amid all this acclaim? The answer is simple: family. "Traditional values are big in my life," she told *Vogue* magazine in 2011. "My grandmother always taught me, 'If you don't have a home, family, and church, you don't have anything.'"

Hudson has all those things and more. This Dreamgirl has already had a dream career. Still in the prime years of her life, chances are that even more "dreams come true" lie ahead.

CHRONOLOGY

1981—Jennifer Kate Hudson is born on September 12 in Chicago, Illinois.

Age 7—Begins singing in the church choir with her beloved grandmother, Julia Kate Hudson.

Age 14—Joins her first musical group, called Final Notice.

Age 16—Gets her first and only "day job," briefly working at a local Burger King.

1998—Julia Kate Hudson passes away; Jennifer vows to make her proud.

1999—Graduates high school and is voted "Most Talented."

—Attends one semester at Langston University before transferring to Kennedy-King College.

—Begins dating James Payton.

—Father, Samuel Simpson, passes away.

2001—Gets a role in a production of the musical *Big River*, which she considers to be her first true professional singing job.

2003—Takes a job as a singer aboard a Disney cruise ship and spends six months at sea.

2004—Makes it to the finals during *American Idol* season 3 and is eliminated in seventh place.

—Tours the United States as part of the *American Idol Live!* Tour.

—Appears on Broadway in a one-night performance of *Hair*.

2006—Appears as Effie White in *Dreamgirls* and wins acclaim for her acting and her rendition of the show-stopping song "And I Am Telling You I'm Not Going."

2007—Wins Academy Award for Best Supporting Actress in *Dreamgirls*.

—Becomes the first African-American singer to appear on the cover of *Vogue* magazine.

—Breaks up with James Payton.

2008—Releases first album, titled *Jennifer Hudson*.

—Appears in *Sex and the City* and *The Secret Life of Bees*.

—Performs at the Democratic National Convention.

—Begins dating and becomes engaged to David Otunga.

—Mother, brother, and nephew are murdered.

2009—Performs at Super Bowl XLIII and wins Grammy Award for Best R&B Album.

—Performs at Michael Jackson memorial service.

—Gives birth to David Daniel Otunga, Jr., August 10.

—Appears in the movie *Fragments*.

—Films an ABC Christmas special in Chicago.

2010—Performs in Hope for Haiti Now concert.

—Becomes spokesperson for Weight Watchers.

—Travels to South Africa to portray Winnie Mandela in the movie *Winnie*.

—Named "Makeover of the Year" by *InStyle* magazine.

2011—Announces to Oprah Winfrey that she has lost eighty pounds.

—Releases second album, titled *I Remember Me*.

—Takes a role as a nun in the movie version of *The Three Stooges*.

2012—Publishes autobiography, *I Got This: How I Changed My Ways and Lost What Weighed Me Down*.

—Performs a tribute to Whitney Houston at the Grammys.

—Attends trial and testifies as William Balfour is convicted of murdering her relatives.

—Takes roles in the movies *Lullaby* and *The Inevitable Defeat of Mister and Pete*.

—Sings Brahms' Lullaby for Pampers.

—Takes a role in the television series *Smash*.

—Launches clothing line.

CHAPTER NOTES

Chapter 1: A Fateful Vote

1. "Interview With Jennifer Hudson," *CBS Early Show*, August 6, 2004, <http://www.cbsnews.com/video/watch/?id=613918n> (September 8, 2012).

2. Jennifer Hudson, *I Got This: How I Changed My Ways and Lost What Weighed Me Down* (New York: Dutton, 2012).

Chapter 2: Finding Her Voice

1. "Childhood home of Jennifer Hudson showcases one of America's most violent neighborhoods ahead of trial in 2008 triple murder," *Daily Mail Online*, taken from AP report, n.d., <http://www.dailymail.co.uk/news/article-2133686/William-Balfour-trial-Jennifer-Hudsons-childhood-home-showcases-violent-Englewood-neighbourhood.html> (January 7, 2013).

2. Nick Curtis, "Oscar Hope Hudson Brings Down the House," *London Evening Standard*, January 25, 2007, <http://www.standard.co.uk/arts/film/oscar-hope-hudson-brings-down-the-house-7207014.html> (September 15, 2012).

Chapter 3: Making Music

1. *Behind the Music: Jennifer Hudson*, Episode 13, June 29, 2010, <http://www.vh1.com/video/behind-the-music/full-episodes/jennifer-hudson/1642519/playlist.jhtml> (January 7, 2013).

2. *The Barry Manilow Official Website*, n.d., <http://www.barrymanilow.com/content/bio.html> (September 2, 2012).

Chapter 4: "An Idol Tale"

1. "Jennifer Hudson's American Idol Audition," *YouTube*, n.d., <http://www.youtube.com/watch?v=aUp1enxZmWU> (September 15, 2012).

2. "Elton John: 'American Idol' is racist," *FoxNews.com*, April 28, 2004, <http://www.foxnews.com/story/0,2933,118432,00.html> (October 2, 2012).

Chapter 5: Dream Role in *Dreamgirls*

1. "Jennifer Hudson: Bringing Down the House," *Vogue*, March 2007, <http://www.vogue.com/magazine/article/jennifer-hudson-bringing-down-the-house/#1> (January 7, 2013).

2. "The Stars of Dreamgirls," *The Oprah Winfrey Show*, November 20, 2006, <http://www.oprah.com/oprahshow/The-Stars-of-Dreamgirls/1> (January 7, 2013).

Chapter 6: Heartbreak and Hope

1. Ari Karpel, "Jennifer Hudson Talks Sex and the City," *Entertainment Weekly*, May 16, 2008, <http://www.ew.com/ew/article/0,,20200581,00.html> (September 15, 2012).

2. "Jennifer Hudson Talks About Her Family Tragedy," *Oprah.com*, February 10, 2011, <http://www.oprah.com/oprahshow/Jennifer-Hudsons-Family-Tragedy-Video> (October 1, 2012).

Chapter 7: Role Model

1. Margena A. Christian, "Jennifer Hudson: Finding Home Again." *Ebony*, December 2011/January 2012.

2. Jason Meisner, "Judge gives Balfour 3 life sentences, calls his soul 'barren,'" *Chicago Tribune*, July 24, 2012, <http://articles.chicagotribune.com/2012-07-24/entertainment/chi-hudson-expected-in-court-today-for-brotherinlaws-sentencing-20120724_1_darnell-donerson-julia-hudson-jason-hudson> (January 7, 2013).

GLOSSARY

adaptation—An altered form; such as a movie adaptation of a play.

apartheid—A system of segregation in South Africa that kept blacks and whites apart.

audition—A tryout, often used in the sense of trying out for a singing or acting part.

contemporary—Of the present time.

crucified—Persecuted or tormented.

dejected—Sad.

diva—A distinguished female singer, often with a big ego.

heinous—Hateful, wicked.

inevitable—Something that had to happen.

intimidated—Frightened, made timid.

ironic—Unexpected or coincidental.

muse—The power that inspires an artist.

oblige—To go along with; be accommodating.

proclaim—To state.

reconcile—To make up with; to come to agreement with after an argument.

recurring—Happening multiple times.

rendition—A version.

renowned—Famous.

speculate—To think or reflect, often in the sense of forming an opinion.

subside—Decrease or lessen.

trauma—An experience that causes psychological injury or pain.

FURTHER READING

Books

Cartlidge, Cherese. *Jennifer Hudson*. Detroit: Lucent Books, 2011.

Hudson, Jennifer. *I Got This: How I Changed My Ways and Lost What Weighed Me Down*. New York: Dutton, 2012.

Snyder, Gail. *Jennifer Hudson*. Broomall, Pa.: Mason Crest, 2010.

West, Betsy. *Jennifer Hudson: American Dream Girl, an Unauthorized Biography*. New York: Price Stern Sloan, 2007.

Internet Addresses

The Official Jennifer Hudson Site
<http://www.jenniferhudson.com/us/home>

IMDb: Jennifer Hudson
<http://www.imdb.com/name/nm1617685/>

INDEX

A

Abdul, Paula, 29, 31, 32
Academy Awards, 51, 55–56, 84
acting
    Dreamgirls, 43–56, 57, 58, 79
    The Inevitable Defeat of
    Mister and Pete, 90
    "Jennifer Hudson: I'll Be
    Home for Christmas," 81
    Lullaby, 89
    reviews, 53–55, 59, 60, 65,
    84, 90–91
    The Secret Life of Bees,
    60–61, 65
    Sex and the City, 59–61
    Smash, 90
    The Three Stooges, 86
    Winged Creatures, 61
    Winnie, 65, 71–72, 82–84,
    90–91
awards, honors, 55–56, 61, 64, 74,
    78, 79, 82

B

Balfour, William, 68, 87–89
Barrino, Fantasia, 5–7, 38–41,
    46, 63
Behar, Joy, 80
Big River, 25
Boynton, Rick, 25
Burger King, 19, 20
Burns, Charles, 89

C

charity work, 69, 82, 91
clothing line, 92
Condon, Bill, 48–50, 55
Cowell, Simon, 29, 31, 32, 33,
    35–38, 54
Creative Workers Union of South
    Africa, 83

D

Daley, Richard M., 57
Democratic National
    Convention, 62
Disney, 25–27
Donerson, Darnell Hudson
    (mother), 11–14, 62, 64–68

F

Fate's Cousins, 19
Fields, Felicia, 25
Final Notice, 18–19
Fitness, 78
Foxx, Jamie, 48, 53, 73
Franklin, Aretha, 10, 32, 35, 85

G

Grammy Awards, 64, 74, 75,
    82, 87

H

Haiti earthquake, 82
Hill, Rufus, 24–25
Houston, Whitney, 10, 33, 37, 52,
    74, 86–87

Howard, Terrence, 83, 84
Hudson, Dorothy, 69
Hudson, Jason (brother), 11,
    65–66
Hudson, Jennifer
    autobiography, 7, 11–13, 15,
        24, 33, 38, 42, 45, 76, 86
    childhood, family life, 8–16
    children, 70–72, 76
    dress style, 14, 18, 30, 31, 36,
        56, 73, 74
    education, 21, 22
    lifestyle, 21–22, 57–58
    murder of family, 65–70,
        87–89
    as parent, 76, 81, 93
    social life, 22, 61–63, 74–75
    wedding, 92–93
    wedding proposals, 62–63,
        74–75
    weight issues, 14, 23–24, 45,
        48, 58, 76–77
    weight loss program,
        77–81, 86
Hudson, Julia (sister), 11, 65–68,
    87–89
Hudson, Julia Kate
    (grandmother), 12,
    15–16, 56
Hudson-King Domestic Violence
    Protection Fund, 69
Huff, George, 6, 39

I

*I Got This: How I Changed My
    Ways and Lost What Weighed
    Me Down,* 7, 11–13, 15, 24,
    33, 38, 42, 45, 76, 86
Imari, 57
InStyle, 78

J

Jackson, Michael, 75–76, 82
Jackson, Randy, 29, 31–33, 37
John, Elton, 35, 36, 40
Johnson, David, 24
Josefsberg, Liz, 77, 81
Julian D. King Gift
    Foundation, 91

K

King, Julian, 66–67, 87–89
Knowles, Beyoncé, 48, 53, 58

L

LaBelle, Patti, 10
Lane, Neil, 75
London, La Toya, 5–7, 38–40

M

Mandela, Nelson, 83
Mandela, Winnie, 65, 82–83, 90
Manilow, Barry, 22–23, 37–38

N

Ne-Yo, 63, 85
Nichols-Sweat, Shari, 21
Nobel Peace Prize Concert, 92
Nunley, Richard, 21

O

Obama, Barack, 62, 67
Oprah Winfrey Show, 52, 78–79
Osbourne, Kelly, 78
Otunga, David, 61–63, 69–70,
    74–75, 87, 88, 91, 92–93
Otunga, David Jr., 76, 81, 90

P

Pampers, 91
Parker, Sarah Jessica, 59
Parton, Dolly, 10

Paul Laurence Dunbar
Vocational Career
Academy, 21
Payton, James, 22, 62
Precious, 58

R

racism, 39–40
Rawls, Lou, 21
Righteous Records, 24

S

Seacrest, Ryan, 5–7, 32, 38, 40
Sidibe, Gabourey, 58
Simpson, Jessica, 81
Simpson, Samuel, 11, 22
singing
    American Idol, 5–7, 26,
    28–43
    "And I Am Telling You I'm
    Not Going," 46–47, 50,
    52–53, 55
    auditions, 22–23, 25, 26,
    29–33, 45–47
    Brahms' Lullaby, 91
    Broadway, 43
    church choir, 8–10, 12
    cruise ships, 25–27
    early groups, 18–19
    eighth grade graduation,
    15–16
    "If This Isn't Love," 74
    image in, 22–24, 30, 31,
    35–36, 45, 64
    influences, 10, 56
    I Remember Me, 84–86
    "I Will Always Love You,"
    10, 87
    Jennifer Hudson (album), 61,
    63–65, 74
    motivations, 15, 33

musicals, 24–25
musical style, 9–10
national anthem, 62, 73–74
nightclubs, 20
recording contracts, 24,
26, 56
reviews, 53–55, 63–64, 86
talent shows, 15, 20
tours, 42–43, 62, 75–76, 86
White House, 82
"Will You Be There?," 76
"You Pulled Me Through," 74
Super Bowl XLIII, 73–74
Supremes, 45

T

Tarantino, Quentin, 37
Thicke, Robin, 75
trilogy workout, 77–78
Twitter, 80

V

Vogue, 57–58
vote splitting, 39–40

W

Weight Watchers, 77–79, 81, 86
Whitlow, Ed, 43
Williams, Walter III, 17–20, 22,
25–26, 28, 30, 31, 43
World Wrestling Entertainment
(WWE), 63, 69, 87